WOMEN EXPRESSIONISTS

To Bernard

WOMEN ◀◀◀◀◀◀◀◀◀◀◀◀
EXPRESSIONISTS

◦ Shulamith Behr ◦

RIZZOLI
NEW YORK

1. Studio photograph of Sigrid Hjertén. c. *1910*

The term Expressionism seems, at one time or another, to have been used to denote virtually the entire avant-garde movement in European art during the period before the First World War. In 1911 it was applied, almost concurrently, to French artists exhibiting in Berlin and to Scandinavian artists—predominantly followers of Matisse—in Stockholm. By 1914, however, the name had acquired well-established connotations within German cultural history, and had extended its frame of reference to embrace music, literature, architecture and the performing arts. In Berlin, Herwarth Walden vigorously promoted Expressionism in his journal *Der Sturm* and his *Sturm* gallery, founded in 1912, was renowned for featuring many international groups. Interestingly, Walden's wife Nell, who was of Swedish origin, maintained close links with women artists in Sweden and Holland. The emergence of notable private dealers within the rapidly expanding urban centres contributed substantially to the increasing independence of women artists.

Strangely, posterity has accorded little recognition to those women who participated in the major Expressionist exhibitions and who assisted the spread of Expressionism. The reasons for this single-gendered view are complex, but include the fact that women artists' avant-garde status was hampered by their conventionally defined role within society, while a persistent and prejudiced critical tradition held the serious matter of 'artistic creativity' to be a predominantly masculine pursuit. It is therefore, perhaps, not surprising that most accounts of modern art have denied women any place within the 'heroic' metaphor. Moreover, even though some of the women Expressionists were well acquainted with one another, they did not, any more than their male counterparts, present themselves to the public as a single-minded, homogeneous group. The artists selected for consideration in this book emanated from different centres: Käthe Kollwitz, Paula Modersohn-Becker, Gabriele Münter, Clara Anna-Marie Nauen and Olga Oppenheimer from Germany; Marianne Werefkin from Russia; Sigrid Hjertén and Vera Nilsson from Sweden; Erma Barrera-Bossi from Yugoslavia; and Jacoba van Heemskerck from Holland. The few 'official' opportunities for art education or for exhibiting their work, must also have meant that these female artists appeared to the wider public as an isolated, even bizarre phenomenon within the modern movement as a whole.

Having been excluded both from the academies and state exhibitions, women artists in Wilhelmine Germany received their training and exposure of their works within specially formed associations (Künstlerinnen-Vereine). Käthe Kollwitz, Paula Modersohn-Becker and Gabriele Münter all pursued part of their initial instruction within such institutions. Due to the unsystematic quality of the formal education and the limited facilities provided by these establishments, many women artists understandably chose to continue their training in studios run by individuals. The private Académies in Paris—Colarossi, Julian and Matisse—also attracted foreign students. Women were gaining admission to institutions at a time when most talented male students were rejecting the fundamental tenets of academicism. The 1890s in Germany, for instance, witnessed the rebellion against the policies of the official exhibiting outlets by the formation of independent artists' organizations (Secessions) in Munich and Berlin.

Even those women who were not restrained from entering the state-run academies in Russia and Holland opted for the alternative: Marianne Werefkin rejected her initial classical foundation at the Moscow School of Art in favour of a ten-year long attachment as a private pupil to Ilja Repin. While there was no direct involvement with the women's movement, the consciousness of 'personal freedom' was an indicator of the debates which centred around the broader, political question of emancipation. These issues are made clear in an unattributed article, possibly by Mrs Ernest Hart, which appeared in the journal *Art for All (Kunst für Alle)* in 1894–5: 'What we women of the nineteenth century demand is that we be freely given all the good gifts of life . . . so that we, as well as the men, . . . can climb the heights of art and science, that we too can enjoy maximum individual development and perfect personal freedom.'

The dominant intellectual influence of Friedrich Nietzsche is apparent in these statements. His hostility towards female emancipation was disregarded in favour of his more general message that no one should any longer be content with the narrow existence which middle-class custom established. Artists, as well as radical exponents of the women's movement, such as Helene Stöcker, understood Nietzsche to be propagating a romantic form of liberalism, emphasizing the conquest of the self and the development of the creative powers of the individual. Such was the substance of Modersohn-Becker's journal entry dating from about 3 March 1899: 'Finished [*Thus Spake*] *Zarathustra*. A wonderful work . . . Nietzsche with his new values—yes, he is a giant. He holds his reins taut and demands the utmost of his energies. But isn't that true education?'

The photographs of a resolute Werefkin standing alongside Alexej Jawlensky in Repin's studio (Fig. 2) and of van Heemskerck seated among her paintings (Fig. 3) display a confident assertion of their identity and professional status. Yet, it was a difficult task for a talented woman artist to achieve both recognition and a socially acceptable image, even among her male colleagues. Otto Modersohn lamented the impact of Nietzsche on his wife and wrote in his journal in 1902: 'Egotism, lack of consideration is the modern sickness. . . . In art, Paula is certainly gifted; I am astonished at her progress. But if only this were joined by more humane virtues. It must

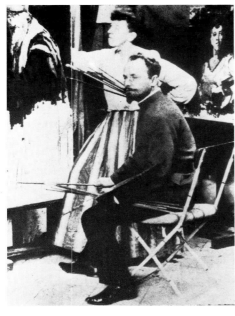

2. *Marianne Werefkin and Alexej Jawlensky in Ilja Repin's studio.* c. *1893*

3. *Jacoba van Heemskerck in her studio.* c. *1915*

be the most difficult thing for a woman to be highly developed spiritually and to be intelligent, and still be completely feminine.'

Arvid Fougstedt's caricature, based retrospectively on his and other Swedish artists' sojourn at the Académie Matisse in Paris in 1910 (Fig. 4), is a visual statement of his own disbelief in the possibility of combining artistic excellence with femininity. Standing in front of Sigrid Hjertén's painting of the nude model, Matisse is depicted extolling the virtues of her work to the group of astonished or attentive male students. Whereas Hjertén is drawn from the rear, almost faceless, elegantly attired and clutching a bag, the other artists are represented either in profile or three-quarter view, some with brushes and palette. Fougstedt, it seems, would have found it inappropriate to have equipped Hjertén with the tools of her profession; possibly her sophisticated appearance (Fig. 1) conveyed such dualities of interpretation. Thus many factors militated against the assumption of independence, and the notion of 'femininity' characterized both the woman artist's ambivalent relationship to society and the dismissive nature of critical reception.

One of the most aggressive categorizations of the role of women in art was published by an art historian, Karl Scheffler, in Berlin in 1908. In contrast to the more benevolent intentions of Ernst Guhl's mid-nineteenth-century publication on *Women in Art History (Die Frauen in der*

Kunstgeschichte), Scheffler's *The Woman and Art (Die Frau und die Kunst)* contended that nature had denied her two of the most essential prerequisites for artistic practice: the 'fanatical forward-driving will' and the 'force that we call talent'. He continued: 'In an Amazonian state there could be neither culture, history nor art.' From the fundamental oppositions that he established—male–female, culture–nature, rationality–instinct—Scheffler concluded that women were incapable of achieving spiritual insights and were more suited to the physical nature of the performing arts. This invective had little short-term effect on the gathering momentum of women artists' self-reliance; the distinctive Women's Arts Union (Frauen Kunstverband) was founded in Berlin in 1913 under the leadership of Käthe Kollwitz. Nonetheless, aspects of Scheffler's sentiments were frequently echoed in critical reviews which, while not totally uncharitable towards the individual, expressed general prejudice against women's productions.

Of Olga Oppenheimer's works included at the Cologne Artists' League in 1910, the critic von Perfall commented: 'Olga Oppenheimer has fallen prey to foreign [influence]. . . . For all that, she brings out a remarkable individual trait in the heads of the double-portrait of a walking married couple and her still lifes can be considered as good decorative works. But her paintings have no intrinsic artistic value.' The qualitative distinction between lesser, 'feminine' capability and 'genuine' creative value is made manifest. To this, von Perfall added the common complaint levelled against the avant-garde: German painters had succumbed to the impact of 'foreigners'.

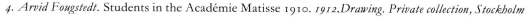

4. Arvid Fougstedt. Students in the Académie Matisse 1910. *1912.Drawing. Private collection, Stockholm*

His suspicions were not unfounded; Oppenheimer had worked in the studio of Paul Sérusier in Paris in 1909 and her earlier two-tone woodcuts, such as the *Rear View of a Model* (Fig. 5) produced in Munich, demonstrate an affinity for decorative contour and the inspiration of the prints of the French artist Felix Vallotton. Her professional activities included teaching drawing and painting from her studio and she was instrumental in creating the Gereonsclub in 1911, a major exhibiting outlet for modern art in Cologne.

These objections were not based merely on opposition to radical formal features, but also on the threat perceived to be directed against German art and culture. That Expressionism, with its international flavour, was often the target for such criticism in the pre-1914 period is understandable in view of the increasing tension in political relations with France. Cultural animosity was absent, however, from critical reviews in Sweden, which initially interpreted Expressionism as the importation of Matisse-like characteristics. For all this evidence, the movement displayed little overall cohesiveness from the viewpoint of style, but received its semantic and philosophical significance from its proponents' shared distaste for Impressionist tenets. Firmly rejecting the documentation of fugitive and external appearances, it favoured the recording of 'events of an inner character'. The restraints of academic training were to be replaced by an uninhibited response towards the medium, which became the vehicle for transmitting the artist's 'inner experience'.

5. Olga Oppenheimer. Rear-view of a Model. 1907. Woodcut, 5 × 4½ in. (12.5 × 11 cm.) Private collection

Generally, the political commitment of Käthe Kollwitz (1867–1945) and her choice of themes—the struggles of the common people, proletarian women, pacifism—have excluded her from the Expressionist canon. Yet, her insistence on conveying psychological realities, such as grief and despair, at the expense of truth to nature, is an accepted hallmark of Expressionism. In a journal entry of October 1920 she elucidated this approach with reference to the print *Memorial Sheet for Karl Liebknecht* (Fig. 6): 'I have as an artist the right to extract from everything its content of feeling, to let it take effect on me and to express this outwardly.' Her eventual choice of a woodcut, a medium that was relatively new to her, for the definitive version of this print was testament to her recognition of the emotional effect achieved by exploiting sharp contrasts and simplified line. A similar though more fluid idiom characterizes Clara Nauen's series of woodcuts which, by virtue of their themes of spiritual transcendence (*Resurrection*, Fig. 7a) and cosmic despair (*Damnation*, Fig. 7d), are more easily accommodated within the recognized Expressionist subject matter.

A resurgence of romantic values and idealization of pre-industrialized conditions led many artists in the late nineteenth and early twentieth centuries to seek a simpler and more meaningful existence in rural retreats. This fashionable 'return to nature' was nurtured by the ideas of writers such as Julius Langbehn and Nietzsche, and led to the pursuit of outdoor activities and an interest in local folk culture. For similar reasons, Münter and Werefkin were attracted to the Bavarian village of Murnau, Nilsson to Öland, off mainland Sweden, and van Heemskerck to Domburg in Holland. During the period 1898–1907, Modersohn-Becker was primarily located at Worpswede, near Bremen, where a regionalist artists' colony had been established by Fritz Mackensen, Otto Modersohn and Hans am Ende.

Modelling herself on the example of the dedicated individualist conveyed in Marie Bashkirtseff's diaries, Paula Modersohn-Becker (1876–1907) benefited from less constraining social attitudes than her earlier nineteenth-century counterpart had suffered. After 1900 she visited Paris on four occasions, her last extended sojourn in 1906–7 being undertaken separately from her husband, whom she had married in 1901. She unfortunately died prematurely at the age of thirty-one, two weeks after the birth of her daughter. With a consistent eye on tradition, Modersohn-Becker's series of figural paintings—self-portraits, peasants, mother-and-child images—exhibit a novel reinterpretation of the realist values established at Worpswede. Her appraisal of the imagery and techniques of the Post-Impressionists led, in her final paintings, to a formal and conceptual statement of primitivism, a notion which was highly important to the ensuing development of Expressionism.

The association of Gabriele Münter (1877–1962) with the Russian artist Wassily Kandinsky has eclipsed the contribution of her sizeable oeuvre. Eleven years younger than him, she was first his pupil at the Phalanx school in Munich in 1901. They became privately engaged in 1902

DIE LEBENDEN DEM TOTEN . ERINNERUNG AN DEN 15. JANUAR 1919

6. *Käthe Kollwitz*. Memorial Sheet for Karl Liebknecht. *1920. Woodcut, 13⅞ × 19⅞ in. (35.5 × 49.6 cm.) British Museum, London*

but never married, and their permanent separation in 1917 severely affected her. In an interview with Edouard Roditi in 1958, Münter reflected on Kandinsky's encouraging influence but emphasized the differences between them. Declaring her passion for 'painting as a form of self-expression', she maintained that, despite frequent incursions into abstraction, she was far more spontaneous in her figurative compositions. A tenacious individuality is displayed in her combination of selected aspects of the genres: landscape, still life, portraiture and interior scenes. As an avid collector of Bavarian folk art, Münter incorporated the naive imagery in her paintings and derived certain formal features from their example. Her contribution to the exhibitions of the New Artists' Association in Munich *(Neue Künstlervereinigung München)* in 1909–10 was substantial and she participated in the formation of the Blaue Reiter group exhibitions of 1911–12. In general, newspaper reviews of her solo exhibitions during 1913 identified her work pejoratively with 'Expressionist' trends in German art.

Münter came into contact with the Russian painters Werefkin and Jawlensky in 1908, when they made frequent excursions to paint in the village of Murnau (see p.38). Marianne Werefkin (1860–1938, Fig. 8) was the daughter of a Russian army family and was encouraged in the arts from an early age. She settled in Munich with Jawlensky in 1896 and, at first, dedicated herself to the furtherance of his artistic career. This self-denial, and the very awkward nature of their relationship until 1920, belies the strength of Werefkin's commitment to art. During this period of non-production she produced theoretical excerpts (*Lettres á un Inconnu,* 1901–5) which reveal

7a. Clara Anna Marie Nauen. Resurrection. *1922.*
Woodcut, 17½ × 13⅞ in. (44 × 35.5 cm.) Municipal Museum, Bonn

7b. Clara Anna Marie Nauen. Spring. *1922–1924.*
Woodcut, 13¾ × 10¼ in. (35 × 27 cm.) Municipal Museum, Bonn

a thorough acquaintance with Russian and French symbolist aesthetics and a formulation of
Expressionist concepts: 'Art is a world-philosophy [*Weltanschauung*],' she declared, 'which finds
its expression in those forms, which inspires its technical means: sound, colour, form, line, word.'
Despite this prescription for abstraction, when Werefkin resumed painting she pursued startlingly
coloured portraits, interior genres and landscapes which invariably incorporated social themes
of peasants and washerwomen. She was a founder member of the New Artists' Association in
Munich and participated in all their exhibitions (1909–12). Apart from contributing to the Blaue
Reiter exhibition at Herwarth Walden's *Der Sturm* gallery in Berlin, both her works and Münter's
were featured prominently in the German Expressionists exhibition held in the same gallery in
1912.

Of all the women Expressionists, the Dutch-born artist Jacoba van Heemskerck (1876–1923)
was predominantly responsible for exploring the implications of abstraction. From 1906 onwards
she based herself in The Hague but spent her summers as a guest of Marie Tak van Poortvliet
at her villa Loverendale in Domburg. Between 1911 and 1913 she exhibited with the avant-garde
group called Moderne Kunstkring in Amsterdam and at the Salon des Indépendants in Paris.
The travelling solo exhibitions of Franz Marc and Wassily Kandinsky, arranged by Walden in

7c. Clara Anna Marie Nauen. Nemesis. c. *1922.*
Woodcut, 17⅜ × 13 in. (43.5 × 32.5 cm.) Municipal Museum,
Bonn

7d. Clara Anna Marie Nauen. Damnation. c. *1922.*
Woodcut, 13⅞ × 9¼ in. (35.5 × 23 cm.) Municipal Museum,
Bonn

Holland in 1912, attracted her attention. The following year, van Heemskerck participated in the First German Autumn Salon and met Walden in Berlin. Her acquaintance with Rudolf Steiner, who was lecturing in The Hague in 1913, inspired her to seek the role of the spiritual in art. After 1915, her Cubist-inspired landscapes were steadily transformed into biomorphic primary coloured abstractions which received an enthusiastic reception from the *Sturm* group of literati in Berlin. Until 1920, van Heemskerck exhibited frequently at *Der Sturm* gallery and promoted various aspects of Walden's organization in Holland, the *Sturm* school of art, stage-group and club.

The so-called Swedish Expressionists also made their début in Berlin in 1915. The exhibition seems to have attracted much attention and the art critic Max Osborn noted in the *Vossische Zeitung* that the young artists, 'are certainly situated . . . surprisingly close to their German and other Expressionist colleagues'. Two of the participants, Sigrid Hjertén (1885–1948) and her husband Isaac Grünewald, had already exhibited together in the new group of Expressionists called The Eight, in Stockholm in 1912. Hjertén's curious linear and spatial distortions in her portraits and studio scenes were based on a theoretical consideration of decorative values, aspects of which were discussed in her article 'Modern and Eastern Art', published in the Stockholm newspaper *Svenska Dagbladet* in 1911. A mental illness curtailed her promising activities in the Swedish avant-garde in the post-war years, but she still continued to paint and exhibit.

The 'wild temperament and the wild technique' of the Öland landscapes of Vera Nilsson (1888–1979) earned her the description of the 'only *one* really consistent Expressionist to be found' in August Brunius's account of the Young Swedish Artists exhibition in Liljevalchs Konsthall, Stockholm, in 1918. Nilsson was largely French trained and had studied at the Académie de la Palette under Henri le Fauconnier during 1911–12, but the works of van Gogh and Munch at the Cologne Sonderbund exhibition in 1912 also had a marked effect on her. She settled in Copenhagen between 1917 and 1920 and thereafter alternated between Paris and Öland. A noticeably liberated woman, she cared solely for her daughter Catherina who provided inspiration for an exhaustive series of single and double portraits. In the 1930s, Nilsson broadened her sphere of reference: she visited the Soviet Union in 1933, and with the increasing threat of fascism in Spain and Germany, her mixed media works and paintings depicted her horror of violence. Her ensuing career was prolific and her works were appropriately featured, as were Hjertén's, in the major retrospective Young Expressionists exhibition at the Nationalmuseum in Stockholm in 1944.

In his book *The Woman as Artist* (*Die Frau als Künstlerin*, 1928), Hans Hildebrandt surveyed the contribution of women artists of the past and present but still maintained: 'Women's art accompanies men's art. It is the secondary melodic part in the orchestra, takes up the themes from the primary melody, modifies them, gives them new, individual colouring, but it resounds and lives [by virtue] of the other.' But the paintings of the women Expressionists were not merely the response to their male counterparts' litany. Indeed, it is ironic that because of the restraints which kept women artists outside the established institutions and because of their changing socio-political status, they were primary candidates for the avant-garde. In paintings, diaries and theoretical tracts, women Expressionists demonstrated their initiative in rejecting the values of official art and questioning the prevailing middle-class attitudes of the time.

8. Erma Bossi. Portrait of Marianne Werefkin. c. 1910. Oil on board, 28 × 22½ in. (71 × 57 cm.) Städtische Galerie im Lenbachhaus, Munich

1

KÄTHE KOLLWITZ

Woman with Dead Child (1903)

Soft-ground etching with engraving,
overprinted with a gold tone-plate
$18\frac{1}{2} \times 16\frac{3}{8}$ in. (47.6 × 41.9 cm.)
Department of Prints and Drawings,
British Museum

The dualities of mothering, those of happiness and despair, were to become central motifs of Kollwitz's oeuvre. She witnessed many tragic events in her husband's surgery in a working-class district of Berlin but it has been suggested that her eldest son's severe illness during 1903 may have provided the thematic inspiration. The content of her work, derived initially from the teachings of naturalism, was thus transformed by personal crisis, a process comparable to Edvard Munch's exploration of a similar theme, *The Sick Child.*

Within a broader context, Kollwitz was aware of the debates in the women's movement concerning the role of motherhood. Proponents of a new morality were more willing than nineteenth-century feminists to accommodate features of women's sexuality. They encouraged middle-class women to marry and to have children while also urging them to seek professional fulfilment. A radical society for the improvement of the condition and status of unmarried mothers was formed in major centres in Germany; Kollwitz donated two drawings (one of which was of a mother and child) to the League for the Protection of Motherhood (Mutterschutzbund) in Leipzig in 1909.

In a dramatic reinterpretation of a *Pietà*, Kollwitz posed herself and her younger son Peter for the preparatory studies for this print. Conceived as a sculptural mass against a gold ground, the lifeless child is depicted as almost devoured by the grasp of the nude mother's body and limbs. Kollwitz had abandoned painting during the early 1890s and had absorbed the impact of the popular etchings of the Prussian artist, Max Klinger. In the stark contrast of printed textures, Kollwitz had clearly internalized the message from his treatise *Painting and Drawing* (*Malerei und Zeichnung*, 1891), in which he had argued that drawing was the true vehicle for fantasy and subjective interpretation in art while painting, by presenting too much definition, left nothing to the imagination.

2

PAULA MODERSOHN-BECKER

Self-portrait on her Sixth Wedding Day (1906)

Oil on board
$39\frac{1}{2} \times 27\frac{3}{8}$ in. (101.5 × 70.2 cm.)
Ludwig-Roselius Collection, Bremen

Life drawing was part of Modersohn-Becker's routine at the Berlin School of Art for Women in 1896. During her visits to Paris, she intensified her study of the nude model and also attended anatomy courses at the École des Beaux-Arts in 1900 and 1906. The combination of self-portraiture with nudity was an interesting departure, and several Gauguinesque explorations of this genre were produced. Painted, in actuality, on her fifth wedding anniversary at a time when she was living away from her husband in Paris, Modersohn-Becker has here represented herself as pregnant although this was not the case at the time. This factor raises several questions concerning her self-image, sexuality and the role of artifice.

Since 1903 Modersohn-Becker had incorporated within her self-portraits the stylized features of the lozenge-shaped eyes and emphatic angularity of the brow and nose that she derived from Egyptian and archaic sources. In this painting the three-quarter-view face confronts the spectator with a level and open gaze. This directness of contact and placement of the partially draped figure against a gently shadowed, floral patterned interior produces a curious conflict between the intimacy of the private studio and the public statement of Modersohn-Becker's nudity. The blond tonalities clarify the upper torso and the enlarged directional brushstrokes focus attention on the distended stomach, protectively encircled by the arms and hands. As in her other works, the gestures establish firm links with traditional prototypes: the connotations of the 'sacred womb' are concordant with medieval and Renaissance interpretations of the pregnant Mary (*mater gravida*), which equally convey a sense of unease in the suggested combination of the sacred and the profane.

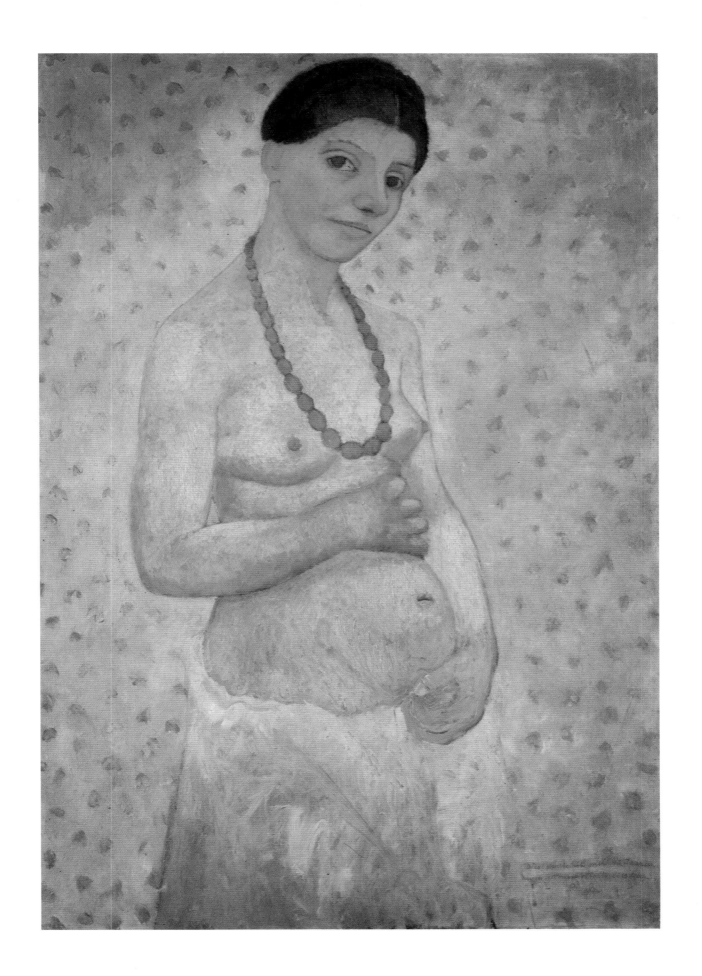

3
MARIANNE WEREFKIN

The Washerwomen (*c.* 1908–9)

Tempera on paper mounted on board
19⅝ × 25 in. (50.5 × 64 cm.)
Städtische Galerie im Lenbachhaus,
Munich

This painting was one of six works Werefkin contributed to the first exhibition of the New Artists' Association in Munich in 1909. The theme of *Washerwomen* was pursued by her in many variations at the time. Whereas the other paintings show procession-like scenes of darkly clad women carrying white bundles, this portrayal focuses on the activity of washing; details of the costume were recorded in sketchbooks of Murnau.

Werefkin's concern for social topics was inherited from her years of apprenticeship to the Russian artist Ilja Repin in St Petersburg between 1886 and 1896. A painter in the tradition of the Wanderers (a realist movement initially associated with radical social comment), Repin included within his subject matter portraiture, landscape and depictions of peasant life. During this early period, Werefkin had concentrated on large oil paintings, predominantly character portraits of Russian peasants, executed in earthy, tonal colours. Comparatively speaking, the *Washerwomen* with its dramatic use of silhouette, distortion and strong coloration has more in common with the rhythmic qualities of the paintings of the Nabis and school of Pont-Aven.

That Werefkin should have continued to think of Repin's inspiration was understandable: he had been a great source of encouragement to her to pursue her career after a hunting accident had crippled the thumb and index finger of her right hand in 1888. The recurring significance of Werefkin's apprentice years in Russia was referred to by Gabriele Münter in an interview with Roditi: 'She [Werefkin] was extremely perceptive and intelligent, but Jawlensky didn't always approve of her work. He often teased her about being too academic in her techniques, and too intellectual and revolutionary in her ideas. He used to pretend that she had never managed to liberate herself entirely from the teachings of the Russian master Ilja Repin. Suddenly Jawlensky would pick on some tiny detail of one of Marianne's best and most original pictures and exclaim: "That patch of colour, there, is laid on much too flat and smoothly. It's just like old Repin." Of course, it was nonsense and he was only saying it to annoy her.'

4

PAULA MODERSOHN-BECKER

Old Peasant Woman (c. 1905—7)

Oil on canvas
29½ × 22½ in. (75.7 × 57.7 cm.)
Detroit Institute of Arts

Apart from depicting the rather melancholy scenery of moors, woodland and the canals of Worpswede, Modersohn-Becker produced a sizeable collection of drawings and paintings based on the theme of the peasant community. Fritz Mackensen had provided the initial inspiration for this subject matter but in December 1902 Modersohn-Becker wrote in her diary that she favoured a less detailed interpretation: 'Mackensen's way of portraying people is not broad enough, too genre-like for me. If it's possible, one should draw them in runic script.' In October 1902 she had emphasized the relevance of 'personal feeling' during the creative process.

The painting of the elderly peasant woman was completed after Modersohn-Becker's fourth and final visit to Paris. It clearly evokes characteristics of the works of van Gogh, Gauguin and Cézanne. The summary treatment of the foliated wallpaper and parapet is a fitting accompaniment to the heavily modelled face and heroic proportions of the woman labourer. Dispelling any hint of sentimentality, a light source from the left illuminates the gnarled features. Paint is applied inconsistently, varying from directional brushstrokes in the shadowed areas of the blue garment to the impasto and chalky texture of the ochre-orange flesh. Black contour plays a major functional role in the definition and simplification of form.

Modersohn-Becker paid homage to the 'great Biblical simplicity' of the Worpswede people and invested these works with spiritual significance. Here the hazy aura around the old woman's head acts as a halo, while the gesture of crossed hands reaffirms traditional associations of the Virgin Annunciate. Whereas the static qualities of this work differ from the tense restless movement of, for instance, an early Die Brücke painting by Ernst Ludwig Kirchner, its direct, primitive force and mystical reference place it most firmly in the Expressionist tradition.

5

PAULA MODERSOHN-BECKER

Kneeling Mother and Child (1907)

Oil on canvas
44 × 28⅞ in. (113 × 74 cm.)
National Gallery, Berlin

Modersohn-Becker's interpretations of motherhood were first noted in her diary in 1898 in Worpswede, where she recorded her impression of a peasant mother suckling a child as an image of Charity (*Karitas*). Soon afterwards she conceived an extension to this metaphor which included the concept of the 'earth mother': 'Frau Meyer, a voluptuous blonde . . . . This time with her little boy at her breast. I had to draw her as a mother. That is her single true purpose.' At that time, Modersohn-Becker categorized the women inhabitants of Worpswede in accordance with her perception of the supremacy of nature within a rural utopia.

In Paris she subsequently returned to this theme in a series of monumental paintings produced during 1906–7. Through the agency of Rainer Maria Rilke, she was introduced to Ellen Key, the Swedish reformer and writer, many of whose books were translated into German from 1902 onwards. Modersohn-Becker's views were possibly confirmed by this meeting; Ellen Key's book *Lines of Life* (1903) included within its first two volumes the sections on Love and Marriage in which she considered the positive and cultural implications of motherhood within the general advance of women's rights.

Although an Italian model was posed for this painting, little evidence of portraiture remains, and the details of the figures are severely generalized. With the emphasis on conveying fecundity, pagan overtones submerge the Christian iconographic referents; plants and fruit, symbols of growth and fertility, are placed strategically within the radically reduced space. Such a formal conception of woman and nature would seem unlikely without the influence of Gauguin's Tahitian works. The exploration of the solidity of form and the primitive features of the mother's head also reflect the impact of Cézanne and African art, the joint sources of early Cubism. Had Modersohn-Becker not died so young, it would have been intriguing to have seen her development beyond this framework of primitivism.

6

MARIANNE WEREFKIN

Self-portrait (*c.* 1908–10)

Tempera on paper mounted on board
$19\frac{7}{8} \times 13\frac{1}{4}$ in. (51 × 34 cm.)
Städtische Galerie im Lenbachhaus,
Munich

By virtue of her military family background, Werefkin's colleagues in Germany entitled her *von* Werefkin. In that she enjoyed both personal and economic independence, she was also incorrectly accorded aristocratic status and referred to as the 'Baroness' (Baronin); her confident bearing and intellectual discourse were considered unusual in the Munich context. Gustav Pauli, an art historian and museum director, recalled Werefkin's vitality in his *Reminiscences* (1936): 'a daintily-built woman with large dark eyes and full red lips,' who, 'on all questions of art and literature, old and new, would engage in debate with unheard-of zeal and just as much spirit.'

Werefkin's *Self-portrait* radiates the intensity and restlessness of her personality. She chose to depict herself theatrically sporting a fitted hat with flower, the startling colour of her piercing eyes being painted with the equally dramatic, red colour. Within the limited flexibility of the tempera medium, Werefkin achieves impasto-like effects in the area of most concentrated attention, around the eyes and knitted brow. Renewed contact with the paintings of van Gogh, at the Kunstsalon Zimmermann in 1908 and at Brakl's gallery in 1909, led Werefkin to adopt from his example the three-quarter-view pose, summarily cut-off composition and swirling gestural brushstrokes. The inclusion of a symbolic light source on the right-hand side of her self-portrait points to her inspirational role. With Nietzschean conviction, Werefkin had prophesied that 'the art of the future is emotional art' and defined her function in evangelical terms: 'People have always come to tell me that I am their star, they couldn't progress in life without me. So, foolishly, I made myself available to serve them until they knew their direction. I held the light of ideals high, I illuminated the way for them.'

7
MARIANNE WEREFKIN

Ballroom (*c.* 1908)

Gouache with coloured crayon
21⅞ × 29⅞ in. (56 × 76.5 cm.)
Private collection

When Werefkin resumed painting after approximately a decade in Munich, she pursued themes of modernity derived from the extremes of social entertainment, from sophisticated salon, ballroom and soirée interiors to scenes from popular culture—the circus, the cabaret and café life. Werefkin visited Paris in 1905 with Jawlensky when he submitted paintings to the Russian contingent of the Salon d'Automne. She viewed the works of the Fauves and was particularly excited by the paintings of the Nabis, Intimists and Odilon Redon. In recording the inspiration of the city and the legendary impact of the Fauves at this exhibition, Werefkin fused her descriptions of art and life in poetic terms: 'It [the soul of Paris] jokes and laughs through the late hours and harsh light of cafés, in front of theatres, on the boulevards . . . Paris and its all-transforming art celebrate their triumph, in insane tones and colours.' After she and Jawlensky had returned to Munich, this direction was reinforced by the visits of the Nabis Jan Verkade and Paul Sérusier to their studio in 1907.

The *Ballroom* exploits the Lautrec-like conventions of the contrasting silhouettes of the foreground couple and rear view of a woman descending the stairs, their elegant forms being delicately defined by arabesque line. The substance of caricature is also apparent in the orange-lit middle ground, where decorum masks the interplay between the old man and the courtesan. Werefkin experimented with different media—coloured crayon and gouache washes of blue in the background—she never returned to oil painting and rarely dated her works.

8
MARIANNE WEREFKIN

The Red Tree (1910)

Tempera on board
$29\frac{5}{8} \times 22\frac{1}{4}$ in. (76 × 57 cm.)
Museo Comunale d'Arte Moderna,
Ascona

The six paintings that Werefkin contributed to the second New Artists' Association exhibition at Thannhauser's Gallery in Munich (1910) were of varied content and featured enigmatic titles, some of which were of symbolist origin. In entitling this painting *The Red Tree*, Werefkin recalled the synthetist aims of Gauguin's *The Yellow Christ* (1889), in which he combined with startling effect his radical theories of vivid coloration with the subject matter of the naive devotion of Breton women. In Werefkin's painting, only a few hints remain of the outdoor experience of nature; a dappled play of light is depicted on the side of the hut. In other respects she focuses on elements of the Murnau landscape in an iconic manner: the dominating, blue, ice-capped mountain; the vivid red foliage of the centrally placed tree; the seated contemplative figure and thatched hut. All these features secure a 'visionary' reading of nature. Certainly Werefkin's concentration on the primary significance of the colours, red, yellow and blue relates to a consideration of their expressive potential.

Both Wassily Kandinsky and Franz Marc were similarly involved with defining the emotional properties of colour. In a letter of 12 December 1910, written to his future wife Maria Franck, Marc, who had just recently become a member of the New Artists' Association, acknowledged the importance of Werefkin's ideas: 'Miss Werefkin said to Helmuth [Macke] recently that the Germans frequently make the mistake of taking light as colour, while colour is totally different and has, in general, little to do with light viz. illumination. This observation has sense, it is very profound and, I believe, has hit the nail on the head.'

9

GABRIELE MÜNTER

Portrait of Marianne Werefkin
(1909)

Oil on board
31½ × 21½ in. (81 × 55 cm.)
Städtische Galerie im Lenbachhaus,
Munich

In artistic communities, such as Die Brücke and the Fauves, members frequently served as models for each other. Münter concentrated on depicting the different personalities in the New Artists' Association and the Blaue Reiter. She had previously painted a double portrait of Jawlensky and Werefkin in a Murnau landscape in which Werefkin had posed wearing the same spectacular wide-brimmed sunhat as here. In this portrayal of her associate, Münter demonstrates her technical command and fluency with codes of expressive emphasis. Against a freely painted yellow-gold ground, the three-quarter-length figure is arranged so as to direct the attention upwards to the head, which is turned towards the spectator but glances sideways. Discordant colour combinations, the largely olive tones of the face reflecting the purple of the scarf, reinforce this compositional focus.

Werefkin was forty-nine years old at the time and the image that Münter conveys presents certain anomalies. Whereas Werefkin's *Self-portrait* (Plate 6), also painted during this period, makes little concession to physical flattery, Münter idealizes the older woman, the casually elegant draping of the long scarf and tipped hat reinforcing a youthful demeanour. Such characteristics of Werefkin's appearance were observed by Elisabeth Erdmann-Macke: 'She was an unusual, vivacious, strong personality . . . . We saw her first as we entered Jawlensky's studio. She was turned away from us, a slender erect figure with glaring-red blouse, a dark skirt and black patent belt, in her hair a broad taffeta bow. One thought a young girl stood there. As she turned round one saw the expressive face, marked by life, of an ageing woman.' Münter preferred to give a rendering of Werefkin's charismatic presence rather than a realistic portrayal. As in many Expressionist portraits, the painting is a self-reflective statement depicting the feelings of the artist towards the sitter.

ERMA BOSSI

Interior with a Lamp (1909)

Oil on board
$9\frac{1}{8} \times 12\frac{3}{4}$ in. (23.5 × 32.6 cm.)
Städtische Galerie im Lenbachhaus,
Munich

Along with Münter and Werefkin, Erma Bossi was one of the women artists who contributed most consistently to the exhibitions of the New Artists' Association in Munich between 1909 and 1911. She painted a portrait of Werefkin (Fig. 8) and was also featured prominently in Münter's interiors of the Murnau period (Plate 17). Few biographical details are known of her, other than that she was born in Yugoslavia in about 1885 and possibly received her training at an art school in Munich. She settled in Paris after World War I and then in Italy. Examination of the catalogue titles and illustrations of her submissions to the Association's exhibitions reveal her involvement with Paris-inspired scenes of modernity, double and group arrangements of women, and with the range of lesser genres so characteristic of avant-garde practice during this period. Bossi shares Marianne Werefkin's interest in the interior scenes of the Nabis and Intimists (Plate 13), and here demonstrates her familiarity with such prototypes. Seated in the lower right-hand corner of this painting, a woman is portrayed absorbed in her sewing. A radical flattening of space occurs as a result of the cut-off composition and over-emphasis on the scale of the lamp in relation to the other objects. The effects of illumination are conveyed, not by tonal values, but by pictorial and decorative use of colour and brushstroke. These avant-garde features and the lack of detail in the silhouette of the woman tend to override any hint of genre implied by the setting.

11

MARIANNE WEREFKIN

Roof-tile Factory (1910)

Tempera on board
41 × 31⅛ in. (105 × 80 cm.)
Wiesbaden Museum

During the period 1908–10 Werefkin and Jawlensky spent part of the summer months in Murnau am Staffelsee with Münter and Kandinsky. At first they all boarded in the Griesbräu guesthouse and painted similar scenes of the streets and environs. With Münter's acquisition of a house in 1909, their imagery was extended to include the view of the Maria-Hilfe church and tower. Inevitably, their works also depicted the encroachment of technology on the Bavarian village: Kandinsky concentrated on the motif of pylons and a speeding train; Werefkin and Jawlensky painted the unexpected intrusion of industrialization on the traditionally romantic Alpine setting. The factory was situated in Oberau, a district not far from Murnau, and its tall smokestack competed with the mountain range to present differing issues to the two artists.

They were seemingly not working totally *en plein air*: Jawlensky produced a series of paintings on this theme and Werefkin worked from a preparatory sketch which is more naturalistic in its planar rendition of detail. Jawlensky's Fauvist-inspired approach, in limiting his range of colours to red, yellow and blue and their tonal variations, is far more decorative and painterly. Werefkin has complied with the same restrictions of palette, but she has compressed the spatial arrangement and deliberately tipped the angles of the main factory and outbuildings, thus producing a very unstable composition. The paint application varies from a stippled, neo-Impressionist handling in the cobblestoned building and haystack to broader areas defined by emphatic dark line. Her inclusion of a figure in the foreground, a feature not evident in the preliminary sketch, is consistent with her practice. As in many of her concurrent works, the image of the displaced peasant was not necessarily based on immediate observation, but relied also upon her examination of the work of other artists, such as Breton scenes by Gauguin and the school of Pont-Aven.

GABRIELE MÜNTER

Boating (1910)

Oil on canvas
$47\frac{3}{4} \times 28\frac{1}{4}$ in. (122.5 × 72.5 cm.)
Milwaukee Art Center Collection

Both Kandinsky and Münter entered paintings entitled *Boating* in the second exhibition of the New Artists' Association in Munich in 1910. Kandinsky's treatment of this subject was decidedly different; his painting (Tretyakov Gallery, Moscow) dealt more expansively with the Murnau landscape, in which the overpowering forces of nature reduced the significance of the small regatta-like boats and their occupants. Münter, in the largest of three paintings in this series, has modified the boating theme, so favoured among the Impressionists for its suggestion of informal enjoyment, into a stark group-portrait. Examination of a photograph from this period (below) establishes the identities of Andreas (Jawlensky's son) in his sailor suit and Marianne Werefkin. Along with a dog, they are compressed into the space between the rear-view self-portrait of Münter rowing the boat and the standing figure of Kandinsky at the stern. By virtue of his position at the apex of the pyramidal composition, Kandinsky's figure has been interpreted as a tacit recognition by Münter of his commanding role—the 'visionary prophet' posed appropriately against a backdrop of the Murnau lake and mountains while she does the hard work. However, Münter's figure controls the manner in which the painting is perceived: the contrived cut-off nature of the boat and her proximity prompts the viewer to adopt her viewpoint, that of the female spectator gazing at the spectacle of the male. In that Kandinsky's glance is unfocused, the intermediary function of Werefkin and the child is to direct the spectator back to Münter's silhouette.

Alexej Jawlensky,
Marianne Werefkin, Andreas Jawlensky
and Gabriele Münter in Murnau
in 1908

13

MARIANNE WEREFKIN

At the Fireside (c. 1911)

Tempera on board
$11\frac{1}{4} \times 15\frac{5}{8}$ in. (29 × 40 cm.)
Wiesbaden Museum

In 1911, a controversy within the New Artists' Association led to the resignation of Kandinsky, Münter, Marc and Kubin and to their planning of the Blaue Reiter exhibition. Although Werefkin shared the ideas of the more radical painters, as is evidenced in this painting, she only resigned the following year after the art historian Otto Fischer attempted to justify the motives of the conservative group in his book *The New Painting (Das neue Bild)*.

In this interior scene, Werefkin's mode of representing the figures and their surroundings is extremely simplified. Colour-washes are peremptorily defined by black line and the faceless, dark silhouettes of the participants are retrieved from abstraction by the graphic emphasis on slight variations of pose and gesture. The composition probably derives from one of the various salons held by Werefkin at her home in the Schwabing district of Munich. Gustav Pauli referred to the significance of these gatherings: 'In this world the salons of the Baroness Werefkin constituted a focal point. . . . Around her table she daily gathered a group of loyal [followers], Russian artists, also the dancer Sacharoff and her Munich friends, a rather colourful group in which the Bavarian aristocracy mixed with the travelling people of international Bohemia.'

It was this cosmopolitanism that prompted critics to rail against the second exhibition of the New Artists' Association in 1910. G. J. Wolf commented in *Die Kunst für Alle*: 'The beautiful and culturally renowned name of Munich is being used as a roost for an artists' association of mixed Slavic and Latin elements. . . . There is not one Munich painter amongst them.'

GABRIELE MÜNTER

Village Street in Winter (1911)

Oil on board mounted on wood
$20\frac{3}{8} \times 27$ in. (52.4 × 69 cm.)
Städtische Galerie im Lenbachhaus,
Munich

During her attendance at the Phalanx school in Munich, Münter encountered landscape painting on vacation courses in the summers of 1902 and 1903, under the guidance of Kandinsky. Her palette lightened considerably due to her contact with French Impressionism when she and Kandinsky settled at Sèvres in Paris between 1906 and 1907. Following their first visits to the Bavarian village of Murnau in 1908, Münter purchased a house there, and the retreat became a frequent venue for gatherings and shared pursuits with their fellow artists, Jawlensky and Werefkin. Münter embraced features of modernism in interpreting the motifs provided by the location—the cluster of houses, wide valleys, lake and mountain range. She also acknowledged the encouragement of Jawlensky in her diary in 1911: 'I have made there [in Murnau], after a short period of agony, an immense leap forwards—from painting nature more or less impressionistically—towards feeling its inner content, towards abstracting and expressing the essence. It was a wonderful, interesting, joyful working period, with much discussion about art with the enthusiastic "Giselisten" [Jawlensky and Werefkin]. I liked to show my works especially to Jawlensky, who advised me, and talked about "synthesis".'

Having spent a short period in the studio of Matisse in 1907, Jawlensky had adopted the term 'synthesis' from symbolist theory to apply to a radical simplification of form and colour in order to avoid anecdotal content. In this painting, the atmospheric effects are neutralized to concentrate on the structural elements of the composition. The major features of the houses and street are reduced to stark contrasts of the white snow and blue shadow, with reddish-pink and green planes being defined by strong use of line. Paint is applied with little nuance in the buildings, contrasting with the scumbled effects of the snow on the unprimed strawboard. Hints of the occupants of the village are provided by the line of washing in the foreground and the black stick-figure following behind cattle in the rear. This painting was included in a group exhibition by *Sturm* artists in Berlin in 1917.

15
VERA NILSSON

Portrait of a Friend—Stina Elliot
(1918)

Oil on canvas
$25\frac{1}{2} \times 19\frac{7}{8}$ in. (65.5 × 51 cm.)
Moderna Museet, Stockholm

After studying art privately, Nilsson pursued training in the applied arts at the Stockholm Technical College between 1906 and 1909. Even though a secessionist movement had started to compete with official exhibiting outlets in Stockholm in 1905, a conservative attitude was still apparent in the policies of avant-garde associations. De Unga (The Young Ones), for instance, a Swedish group to whom the term Expressionist was first applied, only allowed male membership during the years 1909–11. As with Hjertén, Nilsson's Paris orientation was significant and after her first visit in 1910, she spent a year at Le Fauconnier's Académie de la Palette. Her figural studies during this period reveal a forceful Cubist quality. On her return to Stockholm in 1912, she spent a short period with Hjertén and Grünewald but only started exhibiting in 1917, in Copenhagen, on which occasion she was joined by another woman artist, Mollie Faustman.

Stina Elliot was a painter of city scenes and landscapes and often visited Öland where Nilsson spent the summers. Nilsson acknowledged her appreciation of Elliot's modelling for this painting by appending a dedication in the lower right-hand corner. As in Nilsson's other portraits of women friends, girls and children at this time, the sitter is contemplative, with her eyes cast downwards towards her left. Such portraits contrast with her depictions of men, who are usually shown more dynamically or as active in their trade or profession, as in *The Carpenter*. Demonstrating her familiarity with Picasso's primitivist distortions, Nilsson adopted the early Cubist conventions for expressive ends. The simplified and gaunt facial shape is accompanied by asymmetrical placement of the eyes and the lips are portrayed frontally despite the three-quarter view of the face. This dislocation of the features is as startling as the prominence of the head in relation to the summary indication of the shoulders and torso. Nilsson employs a restricted palette of earth tones, varied only by the delicate arrangement of the red bead necklace.

44

16
GABRIELE MÜNTER

Still Life with St George (1911)

Oil on board
20 × 26½ in. (51.1 × 68 cm.)
Städtische Galerie im Lenbachhaus,
Munich

In a deliberate attempt to present images contrary to the modernization that was speedily overtaking Germany, many Expressionists turned to the concept of the 'primitive'. This referred not only to the adoption of motifs and techniques selected from non-Western art but also entailed emulation of the communal life styles of pre-industrialized communities. Whereas the members of Die Brücke predominantly pursued images and the production of objects inspired by African and Polynesian prototypes, Münter and the other artists of Der Blaue Reiter also absorbed the impact of folk art. She first encountered the naive portrayal of patron saints and religious motifs of traditional Bavarian glass-painting (*Hinterglasbilder*) in Murnau and learnt the technique from a local family called Rambold. By 1911, most members of the Blaue Reiter group had experimented with the medium, and Münter had established a substantial collection of folk art which she introduced into her still-life arrangements.

The *Still Life with St George* combines a motley assortment of images: the Madonna statue, small crèche figurines from Oberammergau, a ceramic hen, a vase of flowers and, on the left-hand side, painted in a hazy aura, the glass-painting of St George. Divorced from their original location or narrative sequences, the votive objects are animated by inconsistent effects of lighting and invested with new mythic associations. St George was the patron saint specific to the peasant agrarian and religious ceremonies of the Murnau region, but the motif, as adapted from traditional glass-paintings, was invested with additional significance by its selection for the cover of the *Blaue Reiter Almanac*. Its folk art origins and depiction of the battle against evil were viewed as a suitable image for the messianic aims of the editors, Kandinsky and Marc, who believed there should be a spiritual renewal in art. Münter shared these beliefs but, as this *Still Life* demonstrates, her artistic statement was concerned with objects and their suggestive potential for spiritual expresssion.

GABRIELE MÜNTER

Kandinsky and Erma Bossi at the Table (1912)

Oil on canvas
$37\frac{1}{4} \times 49$ in. (95.5 × 125.5 cm.)
Städtische Galerie im Lenbachhaus,
Munich

Münter first recorded aspects of this table conversation scene in her Murnau sketchbook. With characteristic deftness and linear precision, she seized on the significance of pose, gesture and object within the interior of what had become known generally as the Russian House. Two small oil studies were produced in 1910; this enlarged version was painted in 1912 and exhibited at the Salon des Indépendants in the same year. A critic remarked: 'Mme Münter shows what takes place in a household of a poor vegetarian, and this is not enjoyable at all.' Münter's treatment of this theme was clearly too austere for Parisian taste.

Erma Bossi, an artist and member of the New Artists' Association, is depicted in a listening position, leaning forward with her elbows on the table; the strategically placed milk- and water-jugs act as a visual caesura separating her from the character portrait of Kandinsky, dressed in a traditional Bavarian walking outfit. His raised hand is formalized into a rhetorical gesture which may be didactic but which also directs the viewer's attention towards the glass-painting and folk-art objects immediately above. As the art historian Anne Mochon has observed in a catalogue on the works of Gabriele Münter, the artist effectively transcends the anecdotal incident by means of such innuendo. The rustic setting, arranged so as to emulate local Bavarian custom, belies the rarified atmosphere in which artistic matters were of such importance.

Kandinsky had great difficulty in defining the 'feminine' qualities of Münter's paintings and, in an introductory essay for her major five-year retrospective exhibition at the Kunstsalon Dietzel in Munich in 1913, he resorted to abandoning the issue of gender. While praising Münter's ability, he demonstrated the Expressionist concern for the instinctive by declaring that her paintings were 'free from any trace of feminine or masculine coquetry'.

18
SIGRID HJERTÉN

Self-portrait (1914)

Oil on canvas
44⅞ × 34¾ in. (115 × 89 cm.)
Malmö Museum

Hjertén's *Self-portrait* was painted in the same year that she participated with the Swedish group of Expressionists in the Baltic exhibition at Mälmo, along with other Expressionists from abroad. It was possibly exhibited under the title *Woman Painter* in the Free Exhibition in Copenhagen in 1916. Elements of coquetry appear in the choice of apparel and treatment of her figure: plumed hat, delicate spotted blouse, red bow, emphasized waistband, long fitted skirt. These features convey aspects of Hjertén's femininity consistent with her appearance in a photograph and drawing by a contemporary (Figs. 1 and 4). Whereas the formal conventions of the contrasting red and green colours, decorative linearity and insistence on the two-dimensional surface clearly display her debt to Matisse, Hjertén's self-image is a disquieting one. The figure is depicted in an uncomfortable position; the mask-like face, with downcast eyes, is perched awkwardly on the narrow neck and is forcibly contained within the dominating curved line of the back and elongated limbs. The act of painting is portrayed unconvincingly: in a refined pose, the hand holding the paint-brush dabbles with an unseen canvas. Further references are made to Hjertén's various roles as artist, wife and mother by the inclusion within the studio interior of her son Iván and his toy horse (which also appears in Plate 22). The yellow-green scene in the arched format which frames her head is based on one of her husband, Isaac Grünewald's, preparatory paintings for the decoration of the wedding room in the Stockholm City Law Courts, a scheme that never came to fruition. But Hjertén modifies the imagery of Grünewald's design to conform with her theme, a *maternité* motif on the left contrasting with the ritual performed by the more active figures on the right.

19

JACOBA VAN HEEMSKERCK

Painting No. 25 (1915)

Oil on canvas
42⅞ × 74 in. (110 × 190 cm.)
Collection Haags Gemeentemuseum,
The Hague

Van Heemskerck rarely dated her works and it has been found that, after 1913, stylistic categories are often inadequate criteria for establishing her development. The display of paintings produced in 1915 in her studio (Fig. 3) suggests that she pursued different formal investigations of landscape, tree and harbour motifs within the same period. From 1914 onwards, van Heemskerck abandoned the practice of giving titles to her paintings and drawings, preferring to allocate numbers. As with many members of the avant-garde, she aimed to communicate expressive values by pictorial means alone.

In this particular painting, the landscape, village and figures are clearly discernible. As a result of her training and contact with The Hague school of painters, van Heemskerck's early drawings and prints had displayed an interest in genre scenes of farm life, but any suggestion of allegory in this painting is subordinated to the more radical features of the composition. The directionally hatched brushstrokes and angular definition of planes testify to the impact of Cézanne and the Cubists, yet the powerful effects of colour and repetition of decorative shapes differentiate her works from these sources.

In the exhibitions of the group The Modern Art Circle (Moderne Kunstkring), in which van Heemskerck participated between 1911 and 1914, the works of the French avant-garde, among others, were displayed alongside the contributions of Dutch painters.

20

SIGRID HJERTÉN

The Red Blind (1916)

Oil on canvas
$45\frac{1}{4} \times 34\frac{3}{4}$ in. (116 × 89 cm.)
Moderna Museet, Stockholm

When Hjertén's works were exhibited with the group of Expressionists called The Eight at the Salon Joël in 1912, there was an enthusiastic and positive response to their display of Matisse-like characteristics. Knut Barr of the *Stockholms-Tidningen* praised Hjertén's work: 'The only female exhibitor reached the most beautiful result in her expression of colour.' In 1918, however, press reception was severely critical of the increased radicalism evident in the large Expressionist contingent at the Liljevalchs Konsthall, to which Hjertén also submitted *The Red Blind*.

In this painting, both the academic tradition of the reclining nude and, indeed, the sensuality and luxury displayed in Matisse's post-fauvist works on this theme appear to be the target of parody. The figure, while following the diagonal orientation of the chaise longue, is awkwardly twisted towards the horizontal in order to accommodate the lengthening of the buttocks and heavy legs. Though the positioning of the hand over the groin would signify an attempt to mask nudity, the female spectacle is arranged so as to suggest availability and to allow for maximum viewing. Nonetheless, the primitivizing distortion of her features and violent angle of the woman's head in relation to the neck and body performs the task of neutralizing erotic appeal. Moreover, the intimacy and pleasure-giving associations of a boudoir setting are subverted by the dramatic spatial tipping of the bed, glaring rays of the lamp and drawn red blind, so calculated to clash with the gentle pinks of the interior.

21

JACOBA VAN HEEMSKERCK

Painting No. 23 (1915)

Oil on canvas
$42\frac{7}{8} \times 50\frac{3}{4}$ in. (110 × 131 cm.)
Collection Haags Gemeentemuseum,
The Hague

The seascape and harbour scene had always been popular in the Dutch tradition of the lesser genres. Van Heemskerck spent her summers at the home of Marie Tak van Poortvliet, an avid patron and collector of modern art. Here van Heemskerck came into close contact with the artists' colony at Domburg, who invested their paintings of nature with symbolic values. Mondrian had produced the *Pier and Ocean* series in 1914–15 in Domburg, which reduced the inspiration of the seascape to the interaction of so-called 'plus and minus' signs.

In van Heemskerck's painting, the rhythmic repetition of certain motifs and colours—dark, symmetrically placed trees, inverted white sails on red triangular-shaped bases and mountainous peaks—is enlivened by the contrasting whiplash tendrils of the branches. Van Poortvliet defined the emotional and spiritual significance of these varied linear devices in an article entitled 'The Understanding of the New Art' in the journal *The New Life* (*Het Nieuwe Leven*, 1919–20): the horizontal suggests rest; the vertical, striving; the curved line is yielding; the zig-zag, struggling; the apex of the triangle suggests the attainment of spiritual heights.

Van Heemskerck's paintings aroused much interest when exhibited from 1915 in Berlin at the galleries of *Der Sturm*, and until 1920 her production of woodcut prints, drawings and paintings was distributed through Herwarth Walden's organization. The emblematic combination of animated trees, sailing boats and unattainable peaks became metaphors for the spiritual aspirations of Expressionist poets. Adolf Behne, a long-established art critic and journalist for *Der Sturm*, included reference to van Heemskerck in his booklet *Towards a New Art* (*Zur neuen Kunst*), published in 1915; by late 1916 he had purchased five of her paintings.

22

SIGRID HJERTÉN

Studio Interior (1917)

Oil on canvas
68⅝ × 79⅛ in. (176 × 203 cm.)
Moderna Museet, Stockholm

Shortly after their return from the Académie Matisse in Paris in 1911, Sigrid Hjertén and Isaac Grünewald were married. In 1913 they moved to a large studio in Stockholm. Views of the city from the studio and the interior scenes both formed a substantial part of Hjertén's imagery. In this painting, which was one of sixty-two works submitted to the Expressionist section at the Liljevalchs Konsthall in 1918, Hjertén provides a curious interpretation of the gathering of colleagues.

Her son Iván acts as intercessor and directs the spectator to the over-refined and violet-clad figure of the artist Nils Dardel. While it is possible to identify·the male artists of the Expressionist group, the women represented remain unnamed and appear to be characterized as types. Dardel's partner, the *femme fatale*, is dressed in black, the smiling profile, frenetic detail and sinuous curves of her silhouette dominating the composition. Sharply reduced in scale in the background, but just as intense in the choice of discordant coloration, Einar Jolin sits in conversation with Isaac Grünewald. The portrayal of the woman between them contrasts with the seductive and energetic image of the woman in black.

Hjertén's interest in the expressive function of the pictorial elements may clarify the reasons for her insistence on linearity similar to that of Art Nouveau and the resultant spatial and figural distortions. In her article on 'Modern and Eastern Art' (1911), composition was defined as: 'the consistent simplification of lines in order to obtain the greatest possible expressiveness . . . concentration of the strongest moments of a movement in the part of the figure performing the movement, the supremacy of colour over tone. The movement of a figure is now compressed within the curve of one single line. The curve is the tune of the work and its consistency must in no way be disturbed by the figure. To enrich the subject, further figures are added at an angle to the first but not to the extent that the balance or rhythm of the picture is lost.'

Any sense of rhythmic harmony in this painting however, is severely disrupted by Hjertén's strange imagery—the preciosity of the men and caricatures of the women.

VERA NILSSON

Study, Öland (1917)

Oil on canvas
$33\frac{1}{2} \times 30$ in. (86 × 77 cm.)
Smålands Konstarkiv, Värnamo

During the summer months Nilsson often visited Öland, the largest island off the southeast Baltic coast of Sweden. Her paintings of the terrain date from 1916 onwards and she often returned to the theme during the 1920s. She displayed an interest in the varied locations of the island: in the west, a limestone ridge forms steep cliffs, while much of the central steppe of Öland, known as the Alvaret, is a limestone plateau of heather and sand without counterpart in Northern Europe. Nilsson focused on the sense of power and the quiet desolation of this treeless plain. In this painting the landscape is viewed from two different angles, which has the effect of suggesting both the proximity of nature and an evocation of topography. The resultant distortion of perspective and the adoption of a lower horizon line than expected allows for the depiction of turbulent atmospheric effects in the sky, which is reflected in the earth tones and brushstrokes of the landscape.

Nilsson clearly recalled the qualities of van Gogh's landscapes that she had seen at the Cologne Sonderbund exhibition in 1912. Edvard Munch and a large contingent of Norwegian artists were invited to exhibit by the museum director Richart Reiche and many Scandinavian artists made the effort to attend. It was primarily the impact of van Gogh's works that had a lasting effect on many of the visitors. Of the twenty-six paintings that Nilsson submitted to the Young Swedish Artists exhibition at the Liljevalchs Konsthall in Stockholm in 1918, it was the Öland landscapes that were seized upon as being most characteristically Expressionist. August Brunius, the critic of the newspaper *Svenska Dagbladet*, praised her works for their individuality and ruthless rejection of conventions and continued: 'Give her the most pious and insignificant landscape as subject and she will transform it into an all-absorbing, apocalyptic sight! It is as if an earthquake had shattered the crust of the earth or as if the graves were just about to open to let the dead escape or as if a ravaging world war had swept across the area.'

24

SIGRID HJERTÉN

View of the Locks (1919)

Oil on canvas
$42\frac{1}{8} \times 35\frac{1}{8}$ in. (108 × 90 cm.)
Moderna Museet, Stockholm

From the studio in Stockholm, Hjertén had a panoramic view north of the locks, towards the church of the Riddarsholmen, city hall and public buildings. In a typical inversion of perspective and scale, the scenic elements of the mid-ground and distance are given equal prominence with the almost incidental silhouette of the small woman on the balcony in the foreground. These spatial features and the hatched brushstrokes, which bathe the distant buildings in a pink and yellow light, are reminiscent of Cézanne. Indeed, Hjertén's admiration of Cézanne had led her to publish details of his biography in the Swedish press in 1911. The primary function of colour and simplification of shapes are taken much further, however, and the lock-side streets are populated with a naive rendering of pedestrians, horse and carriage and tram-cars. Apart from the clouds of smoke rising from the train crossing the bridge and from the distant industrial chimneys, Hjertén deliberately primitivizes the modern city. Her concentration on the repetition of decorative detail in the balcony railing and the ethnic motifs in the curtain drape is a characteristic quality of her works. This practice derives from her initial training in the applied arts at Stockholm's High School of Industrial Art. In view of their limited access to the Academy, this was a traditional route for women artists in Sweden to follow. Hjertén's designs for tapestries were extremely accomplished and had received much attention when exhibited in 1909.

An interest in folk and cultural origins was also emphasized by the Swedish Expressionists: Isaac Grünewald issued a manifesto in 1918 entitled *The New Renaissance in Art* in which he proclaimed that: 'The Expressionist knew that he had to create a new language, to cleanse his palette . . . he was a primitive.' Just as Hjertén had indicated in her article on 'Modern and Eastern Art' in 1911, Grünewald favoured the vast range of Eastern and primitive sources in preference to the 'suffocating' qualities of the Old Masters of the Louvre.

25

VERA NILSSON

Two Trees, Amager (1918)

Oil on canvas
$34\frac{3}{4} \times 30\frac{3}{8}$ in. (89 × 78 cm.)
Malmö Museum

Between 1917 and 1920 Nilsson settled in Copenhagen and, apart from painting city scenes and portraits, she produced a series of landscapes at Amager in Denmark. In contrast to the planarity of the Öland terrain study (Plate 23), Nilsson here focused on tree motifs and, in a manner typical of the northern romantic tradition, invested nature with anthropomorphic qualities. Set against an atmospheric red-brown sky, the *Two Trees* contrast in their detailing: the one, dark and distinctly upright and composed, the other, bathed in light, its knotted bough and tendril-like branches evoking the writhing of a human torso and limbs. When this painting was exhibited at the Falangens exhibition in Stockholm in 1922, Erik Blomberg was prompted to suggest that the images were 'moist with anxiety'.

This element of psychological intensity was perceived as a most unusual quality of women's production and, in a critical review of Nilsson's début exhibition in Copenhagen in 1917, Jens Pedersen wrote in the *Social-Demokraten*: 'These works by a woman artist are primarily characterized by their absolute originality and complete absence of the . . . imitative qualities generally encountered in the artistic production of ladies. Vera Nilsson has an inspired, sensitive disposition which goes beyond fashion, fancies and mannerisms but, beyond her proven and sure painting skill, every piece of work is felt and seen afresh and with new eyes as a revelation . . . . The watercolours and drawings are at the same time strange and . . . somehow comprehended in the throat!'

26

JACOBA VAN HEEMSKERCK

Painting No. 105 (1920)

Oil on canvas
39 × 31¼ in. (100 × 80 cm.)
Collection Haags Gemeentemuseum,
The Hague

By 1920 the most important feature of van Heemskerck's paintings was the overpowering effect of colour and its apparent freedom of application. Dispensing with the confinement of quasi-geometric forms, she explored the values of organic and lava-like shapes of vivid coloration, some saturated and others tonally textured. Reference to residual landscape imagery is apparent in the black contoured emphasis on the vertical blue tree, trailing branches and fencing. Van Heemskerck was already aware of Wassily Kandinsky's theories on the psychological and physical effect of colour as outlined in his treatise *On the Spiritual in Art* (1912), but her interest in colour symbolism received further impetus from her circle of friends in Holland.

After viewing her works alongside those of Franz Marc and Kandinsky at the *Sturm* Expressionist exhibition in The Hague in 1916, the architect Jan Buijs introduced F. W. Zeylmans van Emmichhoven, a medical student, to van Heemskerck. They were all actively involved in promoting principles of anthroposophy and Zeylmans immediately wrote an article entitled 'The spiritual direction of the new painting—Jacoba van Heemskerck' (1917). Seizing on colour as being the major factor of her works, Zeylmans asserted: 'Each colour raises a spiritual value . . . whether of conflict or harmony.' Indebted to the theories of Goethe and Steiner, he attributed emotional values to the different colours: red is the colour of violence; green, that of harmony in nature; yellow is symbolic of restless searching; blue is the colour of thoughtfulness, and so on.

It is difficult to assess whether van Heemskerck actively applied these theories to her paintings, but there is evidence to suggest that she and Zeylmans attempted to give scientific foundation to these subjective interpretations. They undertook a series of controlled experiments on children in Domburg in 1918 in order to investigate the emotional effects of different colours, the results of which were only reported by Zeylmans after van Heemskerck's death in 1923.

27

GABRIELE MÜNTER

Reflection (1917)

Oil on canvas
$25\frac{3}{4} \times 38\frac{3}{4}$ in. (66 × 99.5 cm.)
Städtische Galerie im Lenbachhaus,
Munich

With the outbreak of World War I in 1914, Münter and Kandinsky moved to Switzerland. He subsequently returned to Russia, and Münter settled in Stockholm. Through her friendship with Herwarth and Nell Walden, Münter established contact with the Swedish Expressionists, Sigrid Hjertén and Issac Grünewald, and painted a portrait of their son Iván. Separate exhibitions were arranged for both her works and Kandinsky's at Gummeson's Gallery to coincide with their brief reunion in 1916. Despite the evidence of much conflict in their relationship, Münter nonetheless hoped that they would marry once Kandinsky had obtained an official divorce from his first wife. With his marriage to Nina Andrewsky in Moscow in 1917, however, their separation was made permanent.

During this difficult period of transition, Münter created a group of paintings focusing on women in interiors, adopting the themes of convalescence, illness and reverie apparent in the works of Munch, Modersohn-Becker and other Expressionists, such as Erich Heckel. The figures are usually posed in front of windows, reinforcing the contrast between the external world and the confinement or seclusion of the interior setting. Still-life objects are markedly more delineated than during the Murnau period (cf. Plate 16) but their forceful physical presence does not detract from the contemplative mood. The upward glance and gesture of the woman in *Reflection* are sensitively portrayed, with a broadly painted treatment of the high-necked dark clothing. Although her identity remains unknown she must have been important to Münter as her image appears in another painting of this series. As in traditional portraiture, the accompanying objects in this painting provide clues to aspects of time and place. The arrangement of dried corn sheaves is a typically Swedish custom and the inclusion of tulips points to the early spring date of completion of the work.

28

VERA NILSSON

Grandmother and Child (1925)

Oil on canvas
$35\frac{7}{8} \times 30\frac{3}{8}$ in. (92 × 78 cm.)
Moderna Museet, Stockholm

In 1922 Nilsson's daughter Catherina was born. Nicknamed 'Ginga', the child presented in her development a constant source of inspiration for Nilsson's works. Yet, her production, as a result, was not simply reflective of 'domestic femininity'. As a single mother, Nilsson's career as an artist was not subservient to the prescribed role of motherhood within marriage. She maintained a studio in Paris between 1922 and 1925, and her work was continuously informed by her time spent there, particularly from her observations of Renoir's depictions of childhood. However, there is little evidence of his influence in the austere impact of this double portrait. The focus of attention on the psychological interplay between the two characters evokes, in part, the example of Munch. Both artists had participated in the large Nordic Art exhibition in Gothenburg in 1923.

The child's portrait is identifiably of Catherina; that of the grandmother was possibly based on a self-portrait. Although the woman is shown thoughtfully supporting the bowl and the back of the child, there is a strong suggestion of personal containment; her gaze appears to examine the spectator. Catherina is depicted with close observation of a child at play: her attention is directed downwards, not entirely focused on the activity of the hands. Both in scale, colour and youthfulness, her image contrasts with the emphatic silhouette of the ageing woman. Nonetheless, the continuity of generations is conveyed by the equally blonde highlights reflected in the grandmother's greying hair. The categories of opposition are endorsed by the positioning of the two windows behind the figures, the overall geometry being temporarily relieved by the container of red flowers in the foreground.

29

MARIANNE WEREFKIN

Ave Maria (c. 1927)

Tempera on board
$28\frac{7}{8} \times 21\frac{7}{8}$ in. (74 × 56 cm.)
Museo Comunale d'Arte Moderna,
Ascona

At the outbreak of war in 1914, Werefkin and Jawlensky emigrated to Switzerland. By 1918 they had settled in Ascona, Werefkin's financial situation having been severely affected by the cessation of her subsidy after the Russian Revolution. She and Jawlensky separated in 1920 and he subsequently married Helena Nesnakomoff, who was their house help and the mother of his son, Andreas.

In Ascona Werefkin entered into the spirit of the international artistic community and her anthroposophist leanings became more pronounced. While she had established contact with the Dadaists and attended sessions of the Cabaret Voltaire in Zurich, her latter works exaggerated the Expressionist qualities of her pre-1914 paintings. Mystical and religious associations became more prevalent in her themes and titles and, as in the Murnau works (Plate 11), the motifs of steep mountain ranges and hill-top villages of the Italian-Swiss Alps were employed as systematic metaphors for spiritual evocation. The dramatic use of the perspective in this painting is accompanied by animated elongation of the buildings and figures. Women are conversing outside a bar at night while prostitutes, situated in the next doorway, glance towards the priest and the small church façade. His dark form casts an ominous shadow, which contrasts with the vibrant directional brushstroke. Nuance and mystery make a precise reading of the painting difficult—the priest's location opposite the women could imply temptation. Fundamentally, however, Werefkin seizes on the dichotomy between the 'women of the night' and the sacred image of the Madonna and Child surrounded by transfigured light in the distance.

30

VERA NILSSON

Playmates (1926)

Oil on canvas
20½ × 14⅜ in. (52.5 × 37 cm.)
Göteborgs Konstmuseum

After her daughter's birth in 1922, Nilsson produced variations on the theme of the child's development. Some of her paintings reflect the impact of Renoir's attitude towards childhood in which the individual features are subordinated to a classicized treatment of form and sensuous application of colour (*Study after Renoir*, 1924; *Venus*, 1925). In other works, however, Nilsson's stark portrayal of emotional states (e.g. *Crying Child*, 1923) pays little attention to such prototypes. Nilsson explored the extended and double portrait in the winter of 1925–6, when she and Catherina went to Borgholm, the main town on Öland, where Nilsson's family had a holiday home. Due to the bitter weather, she embarked on a series of portraits of models who were close at hand. In one instance, the images of Catherina and her friends, the children of the Wihlborg family, were combined in a horizontal format as a repetition of profiles.

In this painting, Nilsson concentrated on the portraits of Margareta Wihlborg and Catherina. Both children are frontally posed and repeat similar gestures, their right hands on the table. What appears to be the recording of a momentary experience is seen, on closer examination, to be a controlled sequence of contrasts interpreted in a vigorous technique. Colour opposition—the blonde child is dressed in black, the brunette in red—is reinforced by the different directions of glance. Catherina's head is turned as she looks downwards, Margareta's wide-eyed gaze disturbingly confronts the spectator. As with Nauen's painting of a girl (Plate 31), certain features, such as the large foreheads and bulging cheeks, are overstated in order to enhance the characterization and effective presence of the children.

31
CLARA ANNA-MARIE NAUEN

Little Girl in a Blue Apron
(*c.* 1925)

Oil on board
26⅛ × 18⅜ in. (67 × 47 cm.)
Städtisches Museum, Mönchengladbach

Clara Nauen (von Malachowski) was born in Hanover in 1880, the daughter of an officer's family. Between 1900 and 1905 she trained in the studio of Kalckreuth in Stuttgart where she met her future husband, Heinrich Nauen. After their marriage in Dresden they settled in Berlin and thereafter in Brüggen from 1911 to 1931. Both she and her husband were part of the group of Rhenish Expressionists (*Rheinischen Expressionisten*) closely associated with the artist August Macke in Bonn. Along with Olga Oppenheimer, she was the only other woman to have participated in the major exhibition held in the Art Salon of Friedrich Cohen's Bookstore in 1913. Little information is available as to the whereabouts of her early work, but the evidence of her graphic and woodcut production of the 1920s (Fig. 7) points to an engagement with the iconography and formalizing devices of Expressionism.

This painting of childhood indicates that she shared similar attitudes towards portraiture. Apart from the tilting of the head, the figure of the child is posed symmetrically and impinges on the spectator's space. Strong colour contrasts are apparent in the red chair set against the green ground and broadly painted yellow shirt and blue apron. Clara Nauen dismisses the cloying sweetness and elaborate costume apparent in nineteenth-century academic depictions of children. Reminiscent both of the simplified formal arrangement and absence of sentimentalization in Modersohn-Becker's paintings on this theme, the painting makes a feature of the irregularities of physiognomy and clothing. The ill-fitting and dishevelled treatment of the apparel belies the girl's narrow shoulders, thin wrists and small hands. Above all, Nauen's concentration on the lack of prettiness and piercing stare of the exaggerated eyes invests the child with a forceful individual presence characteristic of Expressionist portraits.

32

JACOBA VAN HEEMSKERCK

Painting No. 123 (1920)

Oil on canvas
$42\frac{7}{8} \times 50\frac{3}{4}$ in. (110 × 130 cm.)
Collection Haags Gemeentemuseum,
The Hague

Of all van Heemskerck's compositions, this painting represents an extreme dissolution of identifiable motifs. Varied use of line, irregularly shaped colours and differently textured surfaces hover around an enigmatic coiled centre. A comparison with Kandinsky's pre-1914 *Compositions* is inevitable, yet he provides subtitles, such as *Resurrection* or *Deluge*. In a comprehensive catalogue of van Heemskerck's works, Herbert Henkel has examined her correspondence with Herwarth Walden. A letter from 1920 reveals her continued commitment to expressive abstraction: 'I have again given only numbers. I have maintained my ideas on not giving titles . . . [They] are so offensively romantic, and now one will have at any time hundreds of Springs, Summers, Trees to Liebknechts, Eberts and so on. Colour and line, above all, has its own different language, that will not be fixed in titles.'

It was in this year that van Heemskerck broke the exclusiveness of her contract with Walden. It is possible, that in the postwar climate major differences had emerged. Walden's editorial neutrality during the war was replaced by his joining of the Communist party in 1919, while van Heemskerck intensified her activites in the anthroposophist movement in the Netherlands in response to Rudolf Steiner's public call for spiritual unity.

She had also diverted her attention to creating coloured glass and lead compositions, the technique of which she had perfected by early 1919. Through the agency of Paul Buijs, she received her first commission for the Wulffraat villa in Wassenaar. Inspired by her reading of Paul Scheerbart's book *Glasarchitektur* (1914), she had already in 1914 conveyed the details of her difficulties with the medium to Walden: 'I would very much like to experiment with painting on glass . . . [but] with normal oil-colours the result is not transparent. . . . When one wants glowing, spiritual colours, the time will come when oil-colours and canvas will no longer be suitable.'

SELECT BIBLIOGRAPHY

RENATA BERGER *Malerinnen auf dem Weg ins 20.Jahrhundert: Kunstgeschichte als Sozialgeschichte* Cologne, 1982

FRANCIS CAREY and ANTONY GRIFFITHS *The Print in Germany 1880–1933: The Age of Expressionism* London, 1984

ALESSANDRA COMINI 'Gender or Genius? The Women Artists of German Expressionism', *Feminism and Art History: Questioning the Litany* (eds. Norma Broude and Mary D. Garrard) New York, 1982

JOHANNES EICHNER *Kandinsky und Gabriele Münter: Von Ursprüngen moderner Kunst* Munich, 1957

RICHARD J. EVANS *The Feminist Movement in Germany 1894–1933* London, 1976

ULRIKE EVERS *Deutsche Künstlerinnen des 20.Jahrhunderts* Hamburg, 1983

ROSEL GOLLEK *Der Blaue Reiter im Lenbachhaus München* Munich, 1974

SARAH H. GREGG 'Gabriele Münter in Sweden: Interlude and Separation', *Arts Magazine* May 1981, pp. 116–19

JELENE HAHL-KOCH 'Marianne Werefkin und die russische Symbolismus', *Slavistische Beiträge* vol. 24, Munich, 1967

ANNE SUTHERLAND HARRIS and LINDA NOCHLIN *Women Artists 1550–1950* Los Angeles, 1978

HERBERT HENKELS *Jacoba van Heemskerck: kunstenares van het expressionisme* s'-Gravenhage, 1982

KÄTHE KOLLWITZ *Ich sah die Welt mit liebevollen Blicken* Hanover, 1968

ANNE MOCHON *Gabriele Münter: Between Munich and Murnau* Cambridge and Princeton, 1980

PAULA MODERSOHN-BECKER *The Letters and Journals* (eds. Günter Busch and Liselotte von Reinken) New York, 1983

ROSZIKA PARKER and GRISELDA POLLOCK *Old Mistresses: Women, Art and Ideology* London, 1981

GILLIAN PERRY *Paula Modersohn-Becker: Her Life and Work* London, 1979

SIGRID RUSS, BERND FÄTHKE and HELENA HAHL-KOCH *Marianne Werefkin: Gemälde und Skizzen* Wiesbaden, 1980

GÖRAN M. SILFVERSTOLPE *Vera Nilsson* Uddevalla, 1986

ULRIKE STELTZL '"Die zweite Stimme im Orchester"— Aspekte zum Bild der Künstlerin in der Kunstgeschichtsschreibung', *Künstlerinnen International 1877–1977* Berlin, 1977

LISA TICKNER 'Pankhurst, Modersohn-Becker and the Obstacle Race', *Block* No. 2, Spring 1980, pp. 24–39

WERNER TIM *Käthe Kollwitz* DDR-Berlin, 1980[2]

J. H. VON WALDEGG and D. STEMMLER *Die Rheinischen Expressionisten: August Macke und seine Malerfreunde* Bonn, 1979

MARIANNE WEREFKIN *Briefe an einen Unbekannten 1901–5* (ed. Clemens Weiler) Cologne, 1960

MARIT WERENSKIOLD *The Concept of Expressionism* Oslo, 1984

MARIT WERENSKIOLD 'Sigrid Hjertén som ekspresjonist: En analyse av "Självporträtt" 1914', *Kunsthistorisk Tidskrift* LII/1, pp. 31–43

ACKNOWLEDGEMENTS

In gathering the material for this book, I appreciate the invaluable assistance given by both local and foreign sources. The librarians Jean Walker and Gabi Reinsch at the Goethe Institute in Manchester have been extremely helpful, and the respective curators of the Haags Gemeentemuseum, the Moderna Museet in Stockholm, the Göteborgs Konstmuseum and the Malmö Museer have been informative and responsive to my enquiries.

The inspiration of the exhibition *Künstlerinnen International 1877–1977* at the Schloß Charlottenburg in Berlin and the articles in the catalogue have provided a critical basis on which to examine the contribution of women artists in countries other than France and England. I would like to thank Peter Vergo for his encouragement in this direction and for his useful suggestions in reading sections of this book. The editor, Ruth Maccormac, has also been of great assistance. I warmly acknowledge the sustained interest of members of my family, colleagues and friends in the progress of this enquiry.

SHULAMITH BEHR

The publishers wish to thank all private owners, museums, galleries, libraries and other institutions for permission to reproduce works in their collection. Further acknowledgement is made for the following illustrations:
1, Fig. 6: reproduced by courtesy of the Trustees of the British Museum; 19, 21, 26, 32, Fig. 2; Collection Haags Gemeentemuseum, Escher Foundation; 5: Staatliche Museen Preussischer Kulturbesitz; 15, 20, 22, 24, 28, Figs. 3, 4: (photographs) Statens Konstmuseer, Stockholm; 12: Gift of Mrs Harry Lynde Bradley; 4: Gift of Robert H. Tannahill. The works of Käthe Kollwitz are © DACS 1988.

First published in the United States of America in 1988 by Rizzoli International Publications, Inc.
597 Fifth Avenue, New York, N.Y. 10017

© Phaidon Press Limited, Oxford, 1988

Title page: Käthe Kollwitz. *Self-portrait.* 1924.
Woodcut, proof of state 6, $10\frac{7}{8} \times 14\frac{1}{8}$ in. (27.5 × 36 cm.)
British Museum, London

Library of Congress Cataloging in Publication Data

Behr, Shulamith.
 Women expressionists / Shulamith Behr.
  p.   cm.
 ISBN 0-8478-0963-3 (pbk.)
  1. Expressionism (Art)   2. Painting, Modern—20th century.
 3. Women painters—Biography—History and criticism.
 I. Title.
 ND196.E9B44   1988   750'.88042—dc19   88-5902 CIP

Printed in Great Britain by The Eagle Press, Blantyre, Scotland